Scary States (of Mind)

Horror in Maryland

by Rachel Rose

Consultant: Debbie Felton
Professor of Classics
University of Massachusetts
Amherst, Massachusetts

Bearport Publishing
Minneapolis, Minnesota

Credits

Cover, © Kim Jones, © Jon Bilous/Shutterstock, © artincamera/Shutterstock, and © yaalan/Shutterstock; 3, © TheCraftyCapricorn.com/Shutterstock; 4-5, © Kim Jones and © Jon Bilous/Shutterstock; 6-7, © Eseniy/Shutterstock; 7, © Lone Wolf Photography/Shutterstock; 8, © Jon Bilous/Shutterstock; 9, © Ethan Daniels/Shutterstock; 10 , © Ll Cook/Shutterstock; 11, © Lfink/Shutterstock; 13, © Pixel Doc/Shutterstock and © Donna Beeler/Shutterstock; 15, © Paul Brady Photography/Shutterstock; 16, © gualtiero boffi/Shutterstock; 17, © Nagel Photography/Shutterstock; 19, © Andrew F. Kazmierski/Shutterstock; 20, © ngaga/Shutterstock; 21, © Jruffa, Dreamstime.com/Shutterstock and © Adamsov Studio/Shutterstock; 23, © Steve Heap/Shutterstock; and 24, © Romas_Photo/Shutterstock.

President: Jen Jenson
Director of Product Development: Spencer Brinker
Editor: Allison Juda
Designer: Micah Edel
Cover: Kim Jones

Library of Congress Cataloging-in-Publication Data

Names: Rose, Rachel, 1968- author.
Title: Horror in Maryland / by Rachel Rose.
Description: Minneapolis, Minnesota : Bearport Publishing Company, [2021] | Series: Scary states (of mind) | Includes bibliographical references and index.
Identifiers: LCCN 2020000563 (print) | LCCN 2020000564 (ebook) | ISBN 9781647470753 (library binding) | ISBN 9781647470852 (ebook)
Subjects: LCSH: Haunted places—Maryland—Juvenile literature. | Ghosts—Maryland—Juvenile literature. | Maryland—Miscellanea—Juvenile literature.
Classification: LCC BF1472.U6 R665 2021 (print) | LCC BF1472.U6 (ebook) | DDC 133.109752—dc23
LC record available at https://lccn.loc.gov/2020000563
LC ebook record available at https://lccn.loc.gov/2020000564

For more information, write to Bearport Publishing, 5357 Penn Avenue South, Minneapolis, MN 55419. Printed in the United States of America.

CONTENTS

Horror in Maryland 4

Chessie, the Sea Monster 6

Death Ship 10

The Ghost of Thomas Dance 14

Seriously Creepy Bridge 18

Spooky Spots in Maryland 22

Glossary 23

Index 24

Read More 24

Learn More Online 24

About the Author 24

Horror in Maryland

Maryland is known for its tasty seafood. But some say there's more than fish lurking above and below the water here. Sea monsters roam the bay. Ghosts haunt old warships. And creepy **spirits** float through the shadows.

Get ready to read four spooky stories about Maryland. Turn the page . . . if you dare.

Chessie, The Sea Monster

Chesapeake Bay, Maryland

One evening in 1982, Robert Frew and his wife were watching the sunset over Chesapeake Bay. Suddenly, a large creature rose out of the water. It looked like a giant snake. Could it be Chessie, the **legendary** sea monster of Chesapeake Bay?

Chesapeake Bay

Over the last 80 years, there have been many sightings of Chessie. Reports are often the same. The creature is huge, measuring between 25 and 40 feet (7.6 and 12.2 m) long. Its head is said to be the size of a football. Its snakelike body slithers from side to side.

The last time Chessie was seen in the bay was 2014. When will the creature be spotted next?

A manatee

There are many **theories** about what kind of creature Chessie might be. Some say it is a **manatee**. However, manatees aren't that large and look nothing like snakes.

DEATH SHIP

USS *Constellation*, Baltimore Harbor

In 1799, the USS *Constellation* entered into battle with a French warship. American sailor Neil Harvey was on night watch but fell asleep while on duty. Captain Thomas Truxton was **enraged**. The captain had Neil killed for **treason**. Neil was strapped to one of the ship's cannons and blown to bits!

The USS *Constellation*

The ship saw many battles, but it is now a museum docked in Baltimore. Still, some parts of the ship's past have stuck around. Visitors have seen a glowing blob thought to be Neil Harvey. Others report a ghost in uniform—perhaps Captain Thomas Truxton.

One man met a guide who gave him a tour. Later, he found out there were no guides on the boat that day. However, the man's **description** of the guide matched that of a long-dead watchman!

In 1822, an 11-year-old assistant to the ship's doctor was stabbed to death. A **psychic** has said the boy's ghost is still there. Is the spirit seeking **revenge**?

The Ghost of Thomas Dance

Maryland State House, Annapolis

Important government business takes place at the Maryland State House. But that is not all. Many believe spirits carry out ghostly activities here, too.

One famous spirit named Thomas Dance turns lights on and off. Thomas also opens and closes doors. He sends out blasts of cold air so strong they could knock a person down. Sometimes, he is seen on top of the building late at night.

Maryland State House

Thomas was a builder who worked on the inside of the state house's **dome**. In 1793, Thomas fell to his death over 100 ft (30.5 m) to the marble floor below. No one knows how it happened. Did he slip, or was he pushed?

Why is the ghost of Thomas Dance back? Perhaps he's angry about how he died. Or maybe he is simply trying to finish the job he started.

The Maryland State House's dome is the country's largest wooden dome built without nails.

Seriously Creepy Bridge

Jericho Covered Bridge, Kingsville

The Jericho Covered Bridge may not look scary during the day. But at night, cars have been known to come to a sudden, unexplained stop in the middle of the bridge. Drivers have reported seeing feet swinging from the bridge's beams in the dim light.

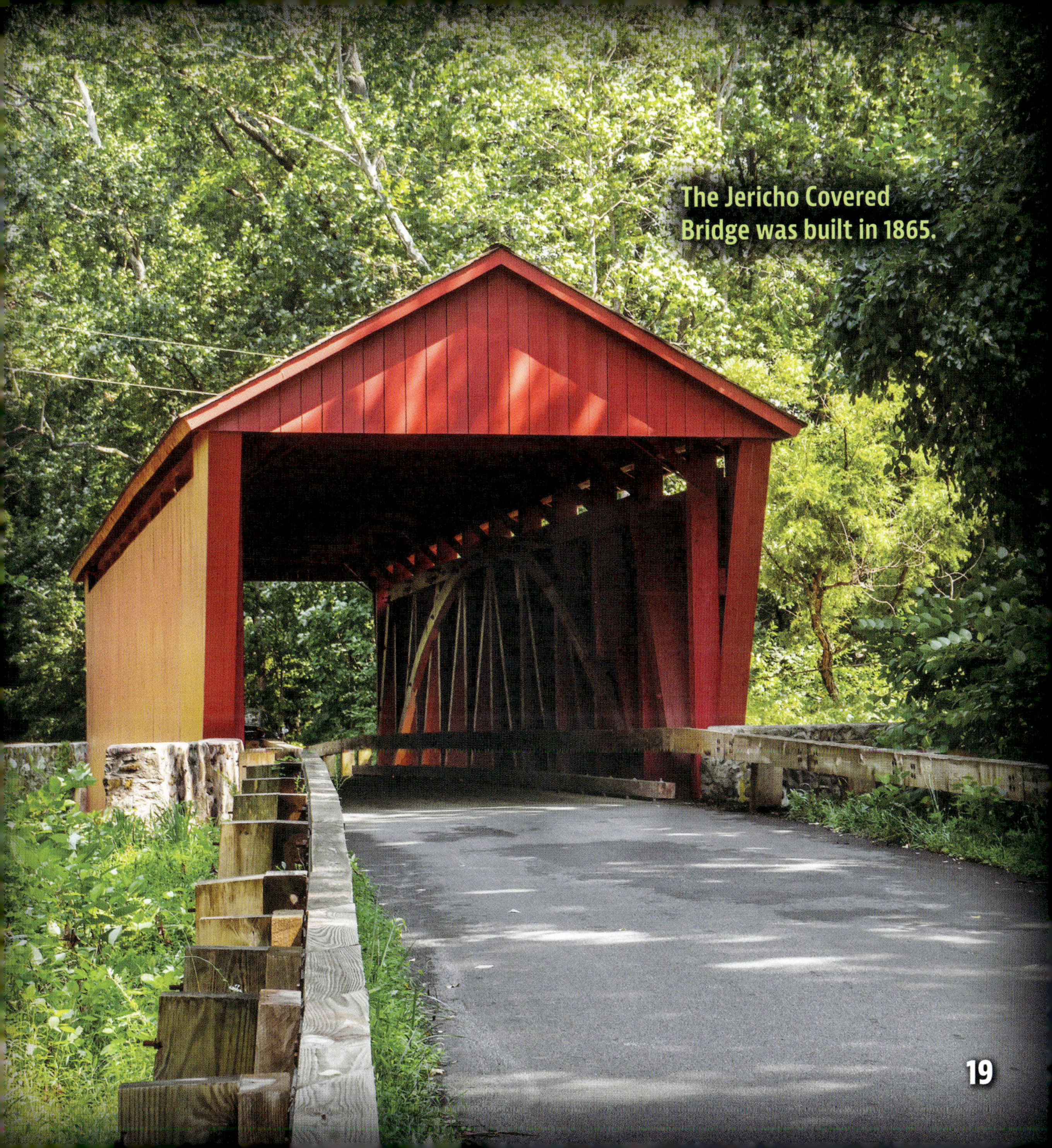

The Jericho Covered Bridge was built in 1865.

Where do these dangling feet come from? Some say they belong to the ghosts of teenagers who hanged themselves decades ago. Others say the story is much older. They believe the feet are those of ghosts of people who were caught fleeing slavery in the 1800s. Still others say former Civil War soldiers killed themselves at the bridge. Whichever story is true, it might be best to avoid the bridge completely!

Some people also claim to have seen a creature with fierce, red eyes guarding the bridge.

Spooky Spots in Maryland

GLOSSARY

description (di-SCRIP-shun) an account of what someone or something looks like

dome (DOHM) the rounded top of a building

enraged (in-RAYJD) filled with anger

legendary (LEJ-uhnd-air-ee) very famous

manatee (MAN-uh-tee) a large mammal found in warm waters

psychic (SYE-kik) a person who can communicate with the spirits of dead people

revenge (ri-VENJ) punishment for something that has been unfairly done

spirits (SPIHR-its) supernatural creatures, such as ghosts

theories (THIHR-eez) ideas that explain certain facts or events

treason (TREE-zuhn) the act of betraying one's country

INDEX

Baltimore Harbor 10, 22
Chesapeake Bay 6–7, 22
Chessie 6–9
Civil War 20
Dance, Thomas 14, 16
dome 16
Frew, Robert 6
Harvey, Neil 10, 12
Jericho Covered Bridge 18–19, 22
Maryland State House 14–16, 22
Truxton, Captain Thomas 10, 12
USS *Constellation* 10–11

READ MORE

Polinsky, Paige V. *Ghost Ships (Investigating the Unexplained).* Minneapolis: Bellwether Media (2020).

Rudolph, Jessica. *Ghost Houses (Tiptoe Into Scary Places).* New York: Bearport (2017).

LEARN MORE ONLINE

1. Go to **www.factsurfer.com**
2. Enter "**Horror in Maryland**" into the search box.
3. Click on the cover of this book to see a list of websites.

ABOUT THE AUTHOR

Rachel Rose lives in San Francisco. She grew up in Ireland and loved listening to scary stories about banshees from her grandmother.